Diamonds of Glory

A Book of Encouragement and Prayer

Erica and Lewis Rutherford, Jr.

Edited by:

ROYSTON
Publishing

BK Royston Publishing
P. O. Box 4321
Jeffersonville, IN 47131
502-802-5385
http://www.bkroystonpublishing.com
bkroystonpublishing@gmail.com

© Copyright – 2017

All Rights Reserved. No part of this book may be reproduced, stored in a retrieval system, or transmitted by any means without the written permission of the author.

Cover Design: Zircona, Glass Diamonds, Noble
Cover Image Zircona, Galss Diamonds Noble | Pixabay
Used with permission and license

ISBN-10: 1-946111-12-0
ISBN-13: 978-1-946111-12-8

Printed in the United States of America

Dedication

We dedicate this book to every man in this hour that needs encouragement, empowerment and strength as they go through life's issues and challenges. Our goal with this book is to bring just that. So this book is for you.

Acknowledgements

First, We acknowledge and give all honor to our Lord and Savior Jesus Christ for giving us all the words to write this book and for gifting us both with the gift to write His words.

To our family and friends that have encouraged and supported us in our marriage journey as we have sought to do God's will in everything that we have done. We will continue to do great things.

Introduction

The Purpose of this Encouragement Book is to strengthen and empower Women who are hurting, misunderstood, discouraged, and going through the twists and turns of life. May this book give you strength for your everyday life, nourish your soul, rekindle the fire in your spirit and renew your mind, so that you can stand in the whole armor of God against the enemy.

Even though Women tend to be mentally and spiritually strong individuals, there is always a need for Women to be encouraged, empower and strengthen for the daily journey of life. God always has his Word available to us in which he uses to speak. Therefore, we want you to read this book as many times as you desire. Take time to read and meditate on the words within. It is our prayer that you will be encouraged and empowered today by God's word. Along with reading your bible, we encourage you to add this to your list of books of encouragement reading. We invite and encourage you to share this book with other women in your life or circle that could use it. We pray God's blessings upon you as you read it and that it would bless your soul.

AND REMEMBER: "YOU ARE A 'DIAMOND OF GLORY.' GOD BLESS YOU.

Day 1

My Best Friend Diamond

Malachi 3:17 KJV
"They will be Mine," says the Lord of Hosts, in that day when I made up my jewels."

Diamonds. Mostly all women love them. They are a woman's best friend. They are beautiful, and they bring out the beauty in a woman. They sparkle and they shine. And that is one of the purposes of a Woman. She too is meant to sparkle and shine. There are two facts about a Diamond. First, they don't start out beautiful. Secondly, they come from deep in the earth. Such is the same as a woman. We come from deep within our mother's womb. We were originally birthed out of the place of the throne room. While, we may not always start out as beautiful, our outside appearance often appears as beautiful. Our inner appearance is that of sin, because of the world in which we were born into. So, the process in which it takes for us to become a Diamond is strenuous. We have to be cut out by a skilled diamond cutter in order for us to sparkle and reflect light. That someone is named Jesus Christ. He is our Master Designer; Our Master Diamond Cutter. Jesus has to mold us and work in our lives, so that we can truly reflect His light within us at maximum power. In order to become that Diamond, there are things that we must do:

D-die to ourselves daily. I-Increase our surrender to God. A-Align ourselves with God's will and purpose for our lives. M-Mediation, praise and worship, read and study God's

Word and make quiet time with God a daily priority. O-Obey God's Word and instructions. N-Never cease seeking God concerning every detail of your life. D-Devote time to working in God's Kingdom in order that others may be ministered to. So Diamond of Glory, how well do you sparkle and reflect God's light?

Prayer Of The Day

Lord, as I am on this journey to becoming the Diamond that you have designed for me to be. I submit myself to you and your process for me. I thank you for forming and crafting me into a diamond that shines and that is full of glory. Now Lord, I ask that you would help me daily to continue to submit myself to your process of helping me to continue to shine. Heavenly Father, let your light shine bright through me that others may know and see you through me. Lord, I thank you for choosing me. I am forever grateful to you. I love you Lord. In Jesus name I pray, Amen.

Day 2

Close The Doors

Philippians 3:13 (KJV)
"No, dear brothers and sisters, I have not achieved it, but I focus on this one thing: Forgetting the past and looking forward to what lies ahead,"

I the Lord, am calling forth the closing of many doors in the lives of my people. I am sending forth my word to you Diamond of Glory, to help you see the door(s) which I desire to be closed. The enemy has been allowed to come in and to destroy the desires, hearts and souls of my people. Through sins, temptations and through false imitations of me. My voice among them has been diminished greatly, and they no longer hear me. But they hear the voices of others. Many of my people have resorted back to the past to try and heal and redeem themselves. They have gone back and pried open doors that I have once closed. They have resurrected people whom I have once cut out of their lives. They have opened the door for them to re-enter their lives knowing what the result will be. Why? Because they have given up on me. They have gone blind, and they have lost their faith. Right now is not a time for being comfortable, but it is a time to press. One must press in order to continue on strong until the end of their faith. They will come against many battles and circumstances that they must fight. Therefore, there is no time to get comfortable. Only I the Lord can give them peace and comfort within themselves. Knowing, that I am ultimately in control over all and that they are not alone and can fight. There is nothing too hard for me to do. Even the more, they can arise with strength and walk in boldness. Knowing that there is nothing that they can't do in my name. I, their God will give them strength and instruction on how to live. So the unsaved boyfriends, the on the side lovers, the family member(s) that seem to be controlling your life, They All Must Go Now. You cannot let them continue to stay. You cannot let them rule and abide in your life. You must close the door once again. You must allow me to be God and deal with them. You must allow me the Lord your God to provide for what you need. Where I have told you 'No' to certain things, you must trust my answer. Continue to trust that I have something better for you. You must understand that even what I am asking you to do right now is for your good. It is healthy, and it is part of my great plan and will for your life. I am removing all unhealthy connections out of your life in order that you may be healthy. Diamond of Glory you can choose this day to return unto me, and allow me to shut those doors in your life. There is a great mandate on your life that I have placed there. I will be with you, and I will help you fulfill it. I need now for you to agree. Will you agree?

Prayer Of The Day

Lord Heavenly Father, it is so hard to close doors sometimes of people in my life. It's so hard to cut off some connections. So Lord, I recognize that I need your help. Please help me to do what I know I need to do but can't seem to do myself. I allow you to fully control my life, because I acknowledge you as Lord. Thank you for closing these doors to restore only positive connections in my life. In Jesus name I pray, Amen.

Erica & Lewis Rutherford Jr.

Day 3

Check Your Armor

Ephesians 6:10-18 (KJV)
"Be strong in the Lord and in the power of His might. Put on the whole armor of God that you may be able to stand against the wiles of the devil. For we do not wrestle against flesh and blood, but against principalities, against powers, against the rulers of the darkness of this age, against spiritual hosts of wickedness in the heavenly places. Take up the whole armor of God that you may be able to withstand in the evil day, and having done all, to stand. Stand therefore, having girded your waist with truth, having put on the breastplate of righteousness, and having shod your feet with the preparation of the gospel of peace; above all, taking the shield of faith with which you will be able to quench all the fiery darts of the wicked one. "And take the helmet of salvation, and the sword of the Spirit, which is the word of God; praying always with all prayer and supplication in the Spirit, being watchful to this end with all perseverance and supplication for all the saints."

Diamond of Glory, each and every day you wake up. Along with putting on your physical clothes and taking care of your physical body, you must also put on your spiritual armor. Each and every day we step outside our home, we mostly have our physical selves together. But what about spiritually and mentally? The Word of God is our daily bread and it is important that we read it every day. It is important that we put on our spiritual amour which protects us spiritually. For the enemy prowls around like a roaring lion, seeking whom he may devour. It's when you least expect it, that you tend to get caught off guard spiritually. That's when we need the greatest protection of all. Mentally, you need to be engaged in what's in front of you and what's ahead of you that sometimes you can't even see. You need to be in tune with the Holy Spirit, who is able to make you aware of all things. So be sure Diamond of Glory, that along with your physical preparations daily that you also prepare spiritually. How? By putting on the full armor of God. That you may be prepared for things to come your way. –Selah

Prayer Of The Day

Heavenly Father, in the name of Jesus. I pray daily that the Word of God would serve as my reminder to put on my spiritual armor, as I put on my natural clothes. Daily as I gear up and prepare for my day, help me to acknowledge you in prayer and to spend a few minutes in your word. Help me to allow every area of my spiritual being to be covered under your blood of protection. Help me to daily be aware of the attacks of the enemy and not take for granted your presence. Thank you Lord for daily covering and protecting me. In Jesus name I pray, Amen.

Day 4

Avoid Bad Company

Proverbs 4:10 (NIV)
"Listen, my son, accept what I say, and the years of your life will be many."

Diamond of Glory, "Do not set foot on the path of the wicked or walk in the way of evil men. Avoid it, do not travel on it; turn from it and go on your way." -Proverbs 4:14-15. We live in a generation where we all want someone to call a friend. We all want that person we can share our life experiences with, someone to encourage us and be there for us. Someone that will have our back, someone to hang out with and etc. God made us with that desire for friendship. God made relationships, because he understood that we would need them. He even tells us in the word to be accountable to one another and to share our faults with one another in order that we may be healed- James 5:16. So God designed us to have relationships. Even as we desire friendships and relationships, we must indeed be careful whom we choose. There are many evil wicked people in earth that seek to do us harm; they mean us no good. We must make decisions not to walk in the ways of nor associate ourselves with those that associate with evil or live evil ways. Diamond of Glory, you are called to a higher standard of living. You are worth more than evil. Diamond of Glory, you are better than that. Good always wins over evil and good portrays the very character of Christ. So Diamond of Glory, will you make the choice to listen and accept God's instructions in order that the years of your life may be longer? Will you decide to make the right choices for your life? Will you rid yourself, if you have not already of the evil men or connections in your life? Make your decision today!

Prayer Of The Day

Lord, help me to examine my friends and connections in this hour. Lord, I choose not to walk in the ways of the wicked nor connect myself with those who practice evil ways. Lord, help me to rid myself and cut off those connections as I seek to live for you. Lord, help me daily to live up to the standard in which you are calling for me to live. Help me in all my decision-making and Lord please place the right people in my life that should be in this season. Thank you Lord for being my best friend. I love you. In Jesus name I pray, Amen

Day 5

Plan and Prepare Ahead

Proverbs 6:6-8 (NIV)
"Go to the ant, you sluggard; consider its ways and be wise! It has no commander, no overseer or ruler, yet it stores its provisions in summer and gathers its food at harvest."

Diamond of Glory, you are like the ant. And the Word of God encourages you to be like the ant. Consider the ant's ways. Ants are small and tiny; sometimes you can barely see them. Though small, they are smart and wise in their ways. One ant usually goes in search for food. Upon finding it, it goes back to its habitat and gets others to come to the harvest. Sometimes it partakes of the food where it finds it, but other times the other ants help carry the food back to its habitat. And they partake of it there. The most important thing to understand about an ant is: that it uses the summer months to begin storing up food. It realizes that winter is coming, and it must store up in order to survive during the winter months. Ants spend their time making the smart choices when it matters, in order to enjoy the harvest in due season. In this season Diamond of Glory, it is important that you consider your decisions. It's important to make sure that provision is made in order to produce a harvest. God when he formed and made you, gave you no commander, no overseer and no ruler. He placed much power in your hand to get wealth. He tells you in the book of Proverbs. That if you seek God for wisdom, that you shall find it and have it.

That if you bind it to your heart, that you shall never be without it. Within God's wisdom, is the answer of how to obtain provision for the harvest that you shall store up. Also, that you are able to gather and partake of your harvest in due season. So Diamond of Glory, will you do what is wise in this season as your progress forward through the seasons. Will you be wise as the ant? –Selah

Prayer Of The Day

Lord, you are my God that loves me and wishes me to prosper in all that I do. Please forgive me for any times that I have been like a sluggard. Lord, thank you for reminding me that I need to be like the ant and be wise in all my ways. Father, you have given me great wisdom through your word. Now, I ask that you would help me to store up provisions while it is summer. In order that I may reap food at harvest time. Help me not to do anything to prolong the harvest any longer. But teach me in order that I may know what I must do to prepare. In Jesus name I pray, Amen.

Day 6

Your High Position Before God

James 1:9 (NIV)
"The brother in humble circumstances ought to take pride in his high position"

To God, your obedience, your sacrifice, your labor, your travail and your dying to flesh is your high position in the eyes of God. God esteems those of us in these places higher than those who operate in pride. Your lowly state is your high place. It's your greatest place. At this level, no man can take away God's favor from you. Not His hand from over your life, nor his blessings that He has in store for you. Nor can they take away His call upon your life, His purpose and provision for you. You are indeed blessed; you cannot be cursed. Where you may had been once last, you are now first. Where you may have been once the tail, you are now the head. Where you may have once seemed to trail through hell, you are already being elevated in the spirit. When it may have once seemed like you were dead, you are already alive. From this place, others will benefit from your experience and will learn of Christ through you. Diamond of Glory, you are moving from your pain to God's promises. You are moving from being weak to becoming strong; from experiencing failures to experiencing successes. Diamond of Glory, you are greater than he that subdues in pride. In the story of Joseph, Joseph in the beginning was sold as a slave. They bruised his feet with shackles and his neck was put in irons, till what he foretold came to pass and till the word of the Lord proved him true" -Psalms 105:16-19. Joseph was being led into a high position. It was there that he was prepared to be the most powerful man in the world as a thirty-year old. He learned many things about God during his captivity that he used later as a ruler over a nation. God's encouragement to you today is for you Diamond of Glory, to find yourself in humble circumstances taking pride in your high position. For the Lord says: "You are greater than he that subdues in pride. You are greater than the arrogant one. You are greater than the fool. Great is your position in my kingdom because of Me. Son, I am pleased to call you mine, says the Lord."

Prayer Of the Day

Heavenly Father. Thank you for helping me to truly understand what being in a high position means. Forgive me for times when I exalted myself in pride before man. Lord, thank you for helping me to become humble and understanding what true humility is. Lord, I am proud to be called your son and I am proud to call you my Father. Lord, help me daily to remain humble and to see all my humbling circumstances and situations as high positions before you. In Jesus name I pray, Amen.

Day 7

Daughter, Don't Give Up On Me

Isaiah 40:31 (ESV)
"But they who wait for the LORD shall renew their strength; they shall mount up with wings like eagles; they shall run and not be weary; they shall walk and not faint."

God's message to you Diamond of Glory today is: 'Daughter, Don't Give Up On Me.' There have been many times that you have been hurt, and many times that you have been deceived. There have been times that you have been greatly disappointed by those in whom you have placed your trust and hope. You may have followed many whom abused you, tried to control you, manipulated you and took advantage of you. But the Lord was still there with you. He cried when you cried. He was angry when things were done unto you. He did not just sit back and watch it all happen. He was behind the scenes dealing on your behalf. There were times when you couldn't take it anymore. There were times you fled away and closed off your heart, soul and spirit. There may have been times that you turned your back on God himself. There were times of confusion when you were wounded, torn and not trusting again. Many times you lost yourself in the process and even lost relationships. Most importantly, your relationship with God sometimes suffered. In response to this, God wants to encourage you 'Today' not to give up on him. He wants you to know that he never intended for you to go through many of the things you went through. He never turned his back on you. He wants you to understand that he was never in the abuse, the hurt, the wounds, the lies nor the deception. He saw what happened to you, and in many situations and circumstances he did protect you. He shall avenge you. He shall take care of those things that concern you. He is continuously behind the scenes working and moving on your behalf. Even in the times that you feel alone and times where it seems like God is so quiet. He shall never leave you. He never forsakes you, and he never gives up on you. And he doesn't want you to give up on him. He is sending encouragement your way 'Today' not to give up on him. You are connected to a God who is love, truth, comfort, healing, deliverance, freedom and peace. He is your strong tower, your avenger, your protector, your Savior and Lord. And he encourages you today to turn back unto him. You will not regret your decision.

Prayer Of The Day

Lord, I am hurting, and I am in need of healing. Lord, I don't know where to turn. You are my only hope. Lord, please forgive me for giving up on you. Lord, please forgive me for not seeking your help. Lord please restore and heal me. Help me not to walk away from you again. Help me to seek after you no matter what happens. Help me to know that you are there always, no matter where I am. I love you Lord. In Jesus name I pray, Amen.

Day 8

God Is Able To Keep You From Falling

Jude 1:24-25 (NIV)
"To him who is able to keep you from falling…….."

In a world where temptation is all around, a man struggles to stay pure and upright. Overcoming temptation is not always easy in a 'right now' society. But God says to you 'Diamond of Glory, 'you cannot overcome alone.' You use your will, your intellect, your prestige and your own wisdom to help make everyday decisions. Your expectation is that the end result will be one of success. But while you may have some success, only one person is able to ensure that you are successful each and every time. That person is Jesus Christ. God's word contains your basic instructions of life. It even contains examples of individuals that dealt with similar issues and situations. Finally, it also contains instructions on how to overcome. But all credit in overcoming any temptation and the continuous battles of remaining in an overcoming state belongs to God. Credit in the book of Judah gives honor and acknowledgment to Jesus: 'To him.' God has all the ability necessary to keep you from falling. Falling from what? Falling back to old habits and ways, and keeping you from retreating back to things that held you bound. What is impossible with you is possible with God. For all things are possible with God. The only one that holds all things in his hands is the one that is able to keep you from going backwards. His desire is that you would continue moving forward. Continue moving forward in life with Christ being your guide. Because of Christ's ability, he also empowers you with his ability and continuous guidance keeping you from falling. Will you Diamond of Glory, allow him to help keep you from falling? Will you give honor and acknowledgment to the one who is able to keep you from falling? To Christ, our only wise God who is able to keep you from falling. -Selah

Prayer Of The Day

Lord, sometimes the battle to stay upright and to not fall is hard, and some days nearly impossible. But I thank you Heavenly Father for your word that says: "I can do all things through Christ that strengthens me." Lord, I need your help to daily keep from falling. So Lord, I honor and acknowledge you now, and your ability to help me. And I receive your help today and each and every day of my life. For I cannot do it on my own. Thank you Lord, for your grace and mercy daily. In Jesus name I pray, Amen.

Day 9

Does Your Devotion Exceed Your Service?

Proverbs 16:2 (KJV)
"All a person's ways seem pure to them, but motives are weighed by the Lord."

"Stay at my feet. Return back to me. Do you think you have all the answers? Do you need me anymore?" Everything I the Lord your God is building up in this hour, is being done with discreet instructions. The key to receiving the instructions is to sit at my feet and learn. Even my son Jesus sought me continuously. He never stopped seeking me; even up to his dying day. Many are serving, but many have lost their devotion to me. In my name, they go forth and try and just ask my blessing on what they are doing. But their devotion to seek me first, is no longer. Many are running on what they think they know and not on my divine discreet instructions. Their heart to hear my voice has diminished. They want only my hand and not my heart. My people have become distracted with service, and they have neglected their devotion to me. Spending time with me has become distinct. Just sitting quietly, mediating without acknowledgment, repentance, worship and communication passes only for the motion of appearing spiritual. The act of seeking me through the mentioned process involves patiently waiting to hear my heart and my voice. This represents pure devotion. Many want my hand and favor, but not the sharing of my heart and instructions. They proceed based on their own understanding. They acknowledge their own ways and direct their own paths. But they try and add my name to it. Just add 'Jesus on it' and you will have a finished product, as though I was only a topping. I should comprise every ingredient, element and layer of your life. Then some criticize those that do seek true devotion or have true devotion with me by saying: 'it doesn't take all that' or 'why do you have to pray about it?'

Why critize them? For they want me involved in as much of if not all every detail of their life as possible. For each of those persons, I am every important in their lives. The element of devotion is real in their lives. So, it is time for my people to cross examine themselves and their lives. You need to ask yourself Diamond of Glory, are you spending time doing service and being busier with stuff, than with spending quality (real) devotion time with me? Does your service exceed your devotion? Where am I on your priority list? Are you moving based on your own knowledge and understanding? Is every action or movement the result of discreet instructions and/or communication and devotion with me? -Selah

Prayer Of The Day

Lord, help me to daily balance my service with my devotion to you. Lord, forgive me for lacking in my devotion to you. I ask you to fix my balance, so that I am not moving according to my own will and understanding but on yours. Help me not to be so busy that I forget about you. Help me to keep you Lord first on my list at all time. In Jesus name I pray, Amen.

Day 10

When Others Fail You

2 Corinthians 5:18: (KJV)
"And all things *are* of God, who hath reconciled us to himself by Jesus Christ, and hath given to us the ministry of reconciliation."

There is a devotional called: 'When Others Fail You' by O. S. Hillman out of the Marketplace Meditations 'Today God Is First Series' that stirs this message to you today Diamond of Glory. The devotion talks about encouraging those around you, that may have seem to fail you when you needed them the most. *The original devotion is based upon the fact that an executive in the owner's company attempted a corporate takeover. But he was unsuccessful in doing so. Afterward, the owner still had to manage the same people who tried to take over his company.* Take time to read it when you get a chance. Today, we are going to look at how Jesus handled his disciples when they failed him as they journeyed with him. Jesus had many experiences with his disciples. Jesus already knew what he would have to endure with them. He also knew the true heart of the disciples. He knew they would flee when he was crucified, and he knew Peter would deny him 3 times. But in the end, Jesus still restored his disciples. Not by focusing on their failures and mistakes, but by building them up to continue on with the mission and purpose that was set before them. In John 20:21-22, Jesus spoke: "Again Jesus said, 'Peace be with you! As the Father has sent me, I am sending you." Jesus used grace and total acceptance as motivation for his followers to carry on the mission. Such was needed for them to be encouraged in their journey ahead. Such was the same with the man who had to continue to work with the employees of his company that failed him in the devotional. He had to rally his team together, and help get them back on track with the vision and goal of the company. He had to build them up even after the failure. So the overall message of this devotional was: WHEN OTHERS FAIL YOU, RESTORE THEM AND SEND THEM FORTH. Wow! What a powerful message. This is what God is saying to you today. The most powerful thing that you can do after someone fails you is to restore them. 2 Corinthians 5:18 says: "And all things *are* of God, who hath reconciled us to himself by Jesus Christ, and hath given to us the ministry of reconciliation." That's what you are called to do, Diamond of Glory. Will you make that choice today, and also allow God to heal and restore you?

Prayer Of the Day

Lord, help me to take heed to your word by restoring my brothers and sisters when they fail me. I realize that life is not over, and that it's not the end of the world. But also Lord, that I still need to be healed. Lord, I ask that you would heal me in order that I may have the heart to restore my brother. Today, I just want to reconcile and not retaliate. Thank you Lord for your example. In Jesus name I pray, Amen

Day 11

Do not Self-Promote, Do Not Run Ahead, But Wait on God.

(Proverbs 27:2)." NETB
"Let another praise you, and not your own mouth; someone else, and not your own lips."

It is crucial in this season and in this hour, that you do not self-promote and that you do not run ahead of God. Don't become anxious for things that you desire and want. Don't become impatient and try to make them happen quicker. Don't try to help God bring to pass the very thing that he promised that he would do for you as though He can't do it himself. Understand that moving and running ahead of God, will only get you in trouble. It will only cause your blessings to become strained. The full manifestation of what God had planned has now become hindered because of your impatience and anxiety. Don't cause yourself to be delayed. Don't risk having to start the process over again because of your own impatience. In looking at the story of David, David's fame was a result of him fulfilling his mission in life. Now David did mess up. But when he failed, he repented and asked for God's forgiveness. And when he was successful, he acknowledged God. Never throughout David's story do you see or find David exalting himself over the Lord. Why? Because David knew better. He knew who was responsible for all his success. He knew who was to get all the glory, honor and the praise. So, the Word of God says in 1 Chronicles 14:17: "So David's fame spread through every land, and the LORD made all the nations fear him." So it clearly noted that 'The Lord' is who caused his fame to spread through the land, and made all the nations fear him. David was just a vessel that the Lord used. So Diamond of Glory, the Lord has a message for you today! Wait on God! Be still and know that He is God. Rid yourself of anxiety and worry. Rebuke the false hunger 'that you have to have this or that right now.' For the Lord is saying: "Yes, This Is Your Time. But let me bring you into your time. Allow me to be your self-promoter. Stand still and know that your gifts, talents and abilities will make room for you in the marketplace and in the kingdom." "Let praise you, and not your own mouth; someone else, and not your own lips -Proverbs 27:2." So Diamond of Glory, Don't Self Promote, Don't Run Ahead, Don't get anxious in well doing, but stand and wait on God. Seek Him and you will never go wrong. Psalms 37:23 says: "the steps of a good man are ordered by the LORD, and he delights in his way." - Selah

Prayer Of The Day

Lord, forgive me for any times that I have promoted myself or ran ahead of you. Forgive me for not waiting on you. Lord, help me to trust you in the process of you promoting me to where you would have me to be. Lord, help me to seek you in everything that I prepare to set out to do for you. Lord, I want you to be in everything. I will let others praise me, and not me myself. I will continuously give all honor to you. Help me in the times I get anxious in well doing to wait on you. In Jesus name I pray, Amen.

Day 12

Your Gift Opportunity

Proverbs 18:16a (KJV)
"A man's gift maketh room for him.."

In 1st Samuel 16:21-23, David was blessed with a special talent of being able to play the harp (lyre). His profession was a shepherd or tender of sheep, which he did in his father's vineyard. In your profession, you may not always have the opportunity to use your talent or gift, but there is always a place for you. At some point in our lives, we will be presented with an opportunity to use our gift or talent. And we must seize that opportunity. David's gift made room for him in his relationship with Saul. He became his armor bearer. David was needed for the very important task of playing his harp every time an evil spirit tried to disturb Saul. The talent of David was used to drive out evil tormenting spirits. David was also especially blessed and anointed by God which added to his success in accomplishing the task. You, Diamond of Glory, have been blessed by God to use your God given talents. And your gifts and talents shall make room for you as well. There is a place and opportunity just for you. Don't be like the man that buried his talents. In Matthew 25:14-38, one of the servants was given one talent. In verses 24-25, that servant hid his talent in the ground. He did not do anything with it like the other servants did. Therefore, his reward in the end was that his talent was taken away and given to the one with ten talents (vss 26-28). Talents back then represented money. Today, talents represent exactly what they are: 'talents.' So the question is: Diamond of Glory, What will you do with yours?

Prayer Of The Day

Lord, Thank you for blessing me with the talents and gifts that you have given me. Lord, you have given me precious gifts and talents made especially for me. Lord, forgive me for not seizing opportunities presented to me to use those talents and gifts. Give me more opportunities. Help me daily to follow your leading and to hear your voice. Help me to continuously be encouraged that my gift will make room for me. Help me not to bury my talents and gifts, but to use them for your glory. In Jesus name I pray, Amen.

Day 13

Chosen for Now

Ruth 2:12-17
(Take a moment to read these scriptures)

The word 'called' means: to ask or invite to come. The word 'chosen' means: selected from several; preferred elect. Diamond of Glory, you have been chosen to fulfill a great purpose in the earth. You are not just called- Matthew 22:14. God knew you from your mother's wound- Jeremiah 1:5. You were chosen for such a time as this- Esther 4:14. Concerning the time in which we are living in right now, you are called and chosen to be an example in the earth. An example of what, you say? An example of how a Woman takes care of her family and her responsibilities. You are chosen because you are gifted. You have purpose. You are one-of-a-kind. You are unique, and you have been equipped with God's favor. Today Diamond of Glory, you must realize that you too must possess high qualifications just as Esther did when she presented herself before the King. How can you know you have been chosen? Because when you have God's anointing and favor upon your life, God also allows you to find favor with men. Look around you and amongst the world. Examine the threat that women pose to men and even those of higher authority. Then, you can begin to understand why you have been chosen for such a time as this. You Diamond of Glory, have been chosen because of who you are. So, Know who you are and walk in your identity as a Diamond of Glory today. Be the example that others can look to. For such a time as this, you have been called and chosen.

Prayer Of The Day

Heavenly Father. Thank you for your encouragement today concerning me. I am honored to be called your child. I am honored and humbled that you have called and chosen me for such a time as this. Now Lord, help me daily to be an example. Help my heart condition daily to be right with you. Lord, take out anything that is not like you. I am reminded daily of who I am because of you. Help me to remember that always. Thank you Lord. In Jesus name I pray, Amen.

Day 14

My Plans For You

Jeremiah 29:11(NIV)
"For I know the plans I have for you, declares the Lord. Plans to prosper you and not to harm you, plans to give you hope and a future."

"For I know the plans I have for you, says the Lord. They are plans for good and not for disaster, to give you a future and a hope." (NLT)

As a Diamond of Glory in this corrupted world, much of what you see around you is evil. There is hardly any good. When you do see good, you try and take pleasure in it; enjoying that moment. For you don't know how long it will last. Tragedy happens every day. Life is running its course daily as God graces you to wake up to see a brand new day. In spite of what each day holds, you should thank God every day and every moment for his grace for you to live and see it. Why? Because tomorrow is not promised. Not even the next moment. Here's what God wants you to know. That in the midst of all that is around you, his plan is to prosper (thrive; flourish) you, not to harm you. The violent and destruction you see around you is not what God originally intended. God's plans for you were plans of peace and well-being. God is a God of peace. And he desires that all have peace. But he also understands that because of the free will of man, peace within the earth is greatly diminished. But in God, you Diamond of Glory can find and have peace and prosperity through God in a time where most people seem to struggle for it. For in Christ, you can find all things that you need. If you seek first the Kingdom of God and his righteousness, then all other things shall be added unto you. So seek God first, the things of God and then the things that you have the most concern for shall be taken care of.

Prayer Of The Day

Heavenly Father, I pray daily that I will be the Diamond of Glory that you have called for me to be. Help me daily to be a Woman of peace and of grace. Help me to continuously seek you for the peace and prosperity that only you can give. I realize that some of the things I see before me is not what you originally desired. But, Thank you Lord for your plans. I am thankful that I can put my full hope and trust in you. Help me to trust your way and will for my life. In Jesus name I pray, Amen.

Day 15

He's Calling You

Matthew 22:14 (KJV)
"For many are called but few are chosen."

In this verse, the word 'called' implies being invited by God to come unto him verses being called by God for a specific purpose. Jesus used this verse as part of a parable titled: "Parable of the Marriage Feast" in the bible. He was simply stating: All are invited to come and follow Christ. But only a few will choose to accept and follow Christ.

Diamond of Glory, God has invited you to come and accept him as Lord and Savior. In this life, you will come to need many things just to survive. Included in those needs, should be your need for Christ as Lord and Savior. Today Diamond of Glory, you have been extended an invitation from Christ to come unto Him. Will you receive and accept his invitation today? Will you accept the invitation to receive the answer to your greatest need? -Selah

Erica & Lewis Rutherford Jr.

Prayer Of The Day:

Heavenly Father, you have taken ordinary people and made them extraordinary. Now Lord, reveal the plan for my life and use me for your glory. Let me be the one who answers the call and lives a life pleasing in your sight. One who lives a life poured out in your service. I receive and accept your invitation today to come. Lord, I receive and accept you as Lord and Savior of my life today. I thank you Lord for the invitation. In Jesus name I pray, Amen.

Day 16

Awaken Your Dreams

Ephesians 3:20 (KJV)
"Now unto him that is able to do exceeding abundantly above all that we ask or think, according to the power that worketh in us."

We as Diamonds of Glory all have dreams of what we want to do. Like owning a business, becoming a teacher; a musician, an astronaut or a lawyer. We know that we need a plan to get there. But often life throws us for a loop, and we settle putting our dreams and the things we want on the shelf. Have we as women ever thought that God has a plan for how we can get there? God wants us to live an abundant life. To accomplish our dreams and the things we want to do. But we as women must believe that he can do it. All it takes is allowing God to help you with it and standing on his word and promise. We must have the faith to know that with God we can do all things. So, awaken your dreams, write the vision, through seeking God set up a plan to get there and watch God help you get there. "The earth is the Lord's and the fullness thereof" –Psalms 24:1. If God said it, He will do it. Why should we as women disqualify ourselves when God says we qualify? For all things are possible to them that believe. So, you can start by having faith the size of a mustard seed, but work on growing to having the faith to tell the mountain be thou removed and be cast into the sea. With that kind of faith, everything we want to do and dream of doing can come to pass. We as Diamonds of Glory must step up to the challenge of awakening our dreams. Then we must allow God to give us the wisdom on how to get there. For if we do the little things, God is more than able to do the big things in our dreams and lives. The start of it is: Believing. Believe that our dreams can come to pass, and that God can help you can do it. Know that it's never too late to make our dreams a reality.

Prayer Of The Day

Father, you said in your word that you want me to prosper even as my soul prospers. So Lord, I pray that every dream and vision you have given comes to pass. Give me the wisdom, the plan, the where and how I get started. Connect me with people who will propel me to my dream, vision and destiny. I stand on your word and promise, and I know you will take care of me. In Jesus name I pray, Amen.

Day 17

You Can't Tell Everyone Your Dreams

Genesis 37:5 (KJV)
"And Joseph dreamed a dream, and he told his brethren and they hated him yet the more."

We as Diamonds of Glory must understand, that we can't tell our dreams to everyone. Even though there will be some who will be happy, excited and proud of us. There are also some who will be jealous and may start to dislike us. Some people will even try to discourage and sabotage us from allowing our dreams to come to pass. Yes. And also try and steal the dreams and ideas that God gave to us. It's important that we women be careful who we tell our dreams to. Why? Because not everyone will be able to handle them. We must use discernment and allow the Holy Spirit to let us know who we can tell them to and who we can connect with. We as women need to surround ourselves with people who will help make our dreams a reality. People, who will build us up and not tear us down, people who will encourage us. So we as men must not allow the ones who are jealous and don't want to be happy for us to get in the way of our dreams. We must continue to move forward in the dreams, vision and ideas that God has given us.

Prayer Of The Day

Lord, help me to be careful to whom I tell my ideas, visions and dreams to. Surround me with people who will be happy and support me, and not discourage and tear me down. Surround me with people, who will build me up and encourage me. Help me not to quit, but keep me working towards the dreams that you have for me. In Jesus name I pray, Amen.

Day 18

God's Love Makes The Difference

Matthew 22:37-40 (KJV)
"Jesus said unto him, thou shalt love the Lord thy God with all thy heart, all thy soul, and all thy mind, this is the first and great commandment and the second is like unto it, thou shalt love thy neighbor as thyself. On these two commandments hang all the law and the prophets."

In the times we live in, 'love' has been a word that has been thrown around. We use the word for other things we love: our cars, suits, houses and other materialistic things. But when it comes to loving people, we're not good at showing it. Two things that Jesus said which summarizes the 'Ten Commandments:' one is to love God with all of our hearts, souls and our minds. Two, is to love others as we love ourselves. The first one is seen like there's no problem in that. Why not love the God who created us and the earth. God, who came down from divinity to humanity, walked among us and taught us how to live. Out of love for us, he freely gave his life for us. He destroyed the very thing that separated us, so that we could commune with him. But when it comes to loving each other the same way that Christ loves us, we fail at that. How is it that we can say 'We Love God,' but can't say two words to each other? We're so quick to dislike, despise and judge. We think we can read people so quick. We put them in a category without taking the time to get to know who they are, and what they have been through. We can't even say a kind word to each other. We are quick to make judgments on another's appearance, knowledge or success. It is amazing how we say 'we're the hands and feet of God,' but we do more hurt and harm instead of lending a helping hand. It's amazing how we as women say we are 'the light of the world.' Yet instead of being a light to a darkened world in these dark times, we choose to stay only among other lights. Lights are meant to illuminate places that are dark. Which means they are spread out. We do a lot of talking, but not enough doing. Always concentrating on looking good, but not being good. God wants us to start being good and not just looking good. For we as women should not only be hearers of the word, but also doers too. So Diamonds of Glory, it is time for us to step up to the challenge. Show others the love of God, and let his love make the difference. Will you be a true example of his love today?

Prayer Of The Day

Father, let your love be in me that I may be a reflection of you. Let when others see me, that they see you, Jesus. Help me to be the woman that loves others and loves my enemies. Allow your love to make such a difference in my life, that it changes the lives of others. In Jesus name I pray, Amen.

Day 19

What Is Your Battle Plan?

Isaiah 8:9
"Devise a plan, but it will be thwarted; State a proposal, but it will not stand, For God is with us."

As you go through each and every day of your life, it is imperative that you have a battle plan on how to conquer the day that's before you. Before you each day, are tasks to be accomplished. For each task at hand, you must have a strategy on how you will approach and accomplish it. In order to devise your strategy, you must have a battle plan of how you will accomplish that task. Spending time in prayer and the Word of God becomes an important element of seeking out and developing a battle plan. Putting God 1st in everything puts you in a position of surrendering onto him yourself and the very task ahead. You are literally inviting him to be involved. Then reading the Word of God and listening to God, helps you to receive the battle plan consisting of instructions on how to move forward. After implementing the strategy of prayer, bible reading and spending time listening to God, your end result is an executable battle. Whatever the battle plan is, follow the instructions to the letter to ensure success. When God's stamp of approval is on whatever it is you are doing, you can ensure that it will always be successful. So Diamond of Glory, what is your strategy for receiving your battle plans for conquering your task(s) ahead?

Prayer Of The Day

Lord, this day. I lay all of my plans and tasks before you. Everything that is before me today, I present them before you. Nothing is hidden. Heavenly Father, I come seeking you first, that I may be in your will. I also need your favor to go before me. I also receive your instructions to follow, and I will obey them. I trust your leading Lord. Thank you for guiding me in executing the Battle Plan. I give you all praise. In Jesus name I pray, Amen.

Day 20

Moving Forward or Staying Stuck

Job 17:9 "The righteous keep moving forward and those with clean hands become strong and stronger." (NLT.)

Each and every day, we are presented opportunities to make choices. God graces us with freewill which includes opportunities to make choices or decisions regarding the who, what, when, where and how. And what a great opportunity we have been given. As we make our choices or decisions, there are consequences that come with those choices or decisions. That consequence may result in our world being shaken to the point that it brings us to a low point or stops us dead in our tracks. Even in that moment, we are yet even given another opportunity to make a decision or choice. That choice or decision is: Will we move forward or will we remain stuck? When death comes, we sometimes remain stuck in the grieving process. We allow our lives to stop, never pick back up again or will even find the courage to go on. Will we take our time to grieve, but then grab ahold of courage and strength to move forward with our lives? This decision or choice can be hard if one does not know Christ. For if your belief and hope is in Christ, then his Word tells us in Job 17:9, "The righteous keep moving forward and those with clean hands become strong and stronger" -NLT. Diamond of Glory that is what you must do in this hour. No matter what comes before you. No matter what tries to shake you or distract you off your path. You must decide to keep moving forward and not to remain stuck. You must find and grab ahold to the hope of God's word. This is in order that you may be encouraged and inspired to keep moving forward daily. You can do it. You can make it. Don't give up and don't give in. Keep Moving Forward, Diamond of Glory.

Prayer Of The Day

Lord, at this moment, I am struggling to move forward. I need your help. I am crying out to you for the strength and hope that I need to go on. I am encouraged by your word that encourages me to move forward and not to remain stuck. By faith, I grab on to hope and strength, and I go forward. Thank you Lord for hearing my prayer. In Jesus name I pray, Amen.

Day 21

Here's My Cup Lord

Matthew 25:35
"I was thirsty and you gave me drink….."

Think about a cup you use on a regular basis. A coffee cup, tea cup or hot chocolate cup. Is your cup empty, half full or completely full? What ingredients comprise your cup: sugar, creamer, milk, ice, sweetener, marshmallows, cinnamon or etc.? What is the temperature of your cup: hot, cold, iced or room temperature? Are you completely empty, wanting God to fill you up? Perhaps, nothing is in your cup. Maybe you are dry and desiring to be filled up. Maybe your cup already contains your favorite drink, but your drink is plain or bland? Is it accompanied by your favorite ingredients? Maybe you are half full or completely full almost to the point of overflowing. If you are half full, do you find yourself desiring more? Or are you still experiencing an emptiness or void desiring to be filled? Do you feel like you are still missing something? Being completely full, are you still longing fulfillment? Do you still feel a void? Are you too full that God can't fill you up? With what? Perhaps, you should empty out your cup and present and empty cup before God.

A cup is a container that must be continuously emptied to make room for new things. Diamond of Glory, you are that cup. You must take time to examine your cup. For if you are thirsty, Your Heavenly Father is able to give you drink. So examine your cup, and allow God to fill your cup with all the right ingredients in order that you won't thirsty again. Come onto the one that is able to fill you up.

Prayer Of The Day

Heavenly Father. Here is my cup. I am thirsty, and I stand in need of being filled up. In spite of the ingredients already in my cup, my soul still feels empty. Lord, I need you to fill that void. Satisfy my soul with more of you. Fill Me Up. Hear My Heart's Cry Now Lord. I surrender my cup to you. Lord, Here's My Cup. In Jesus name I pray, Amen.

Day 22

Come, Have A Drink At The Well

John 4:14
"But whoever drinks of the water that I shall give him will never thirst. But the water that I shall give him will become in him a fountain of water springing up into everlasting life."

Diamond of Glory, it's time for you to make a stop by the well. It's time for some alone time with God. He is waiting on you. He is anticipating your arrival. He knows you long for a drink. He wants to fill you up. In John 4:4-26, Jesus talks to a Woman at the Well. While the woman thinks she is at the well just to get a drink, she encounters Jesus whom she comes to find out knows all about her. He is about to tell her distinct details about her life and current situation. Part of the conclusion of this story, she was able to go back and tells others about Jesus whom she had encountered at the well. She had an encounter with a Man that was able to quench her thirst, so that she would never thirst again. Jesus today, wants to do the same with you. You don't have to go another day the same way. You too can meet Jesus at the Well. While the well might seem to be the most odds place to meet Jesus, it was the most life changing place. This lets you know that Jesus is able to meet you at any point in your life. There is never a place where Jesus won't meet us. How about you, Diamond of Glory? Come and meet him today. He is awaiting your arrival.

Erica & Lewis Rutherford Jr.

Prayer Of The Day

Heavenly Father. I come before you right now, because I need a drink from the well. I need an encounter with you. Lord, come nigh and hear my prayer. Lord, I know that you are always near and waiting. Lord. I need to be filled with your everlasting water. Please quench the thirsting in my soul. Thank you Lord for meeting me today. I appreciate our time together. In Jesus name I pray, Amen.

Day 23

You're Next In Line

Esther 4:14
Adding Your Name To The Bloodline.

Yes. Today, Diamond of Glory. You are Next in Line. To be sent forth, to be elevated, to receive your next assignment and to be catapulted into another dimension. Yes You. You have waited a long time. You have labored but have seen all others pass you up. You have celebrated others as they reached their time. Now, it's your time. It's time to add your name to the Bloodline of Women whom have in obedience marched forward and continued the Work of the Kingdom. Women whom have fought the good fight of faith, and whom have served the Lord till the end. Your name is now being added to a Bloodline of Women, whom have proceeded you in doing what you are about to now do. Your time has come. Are you ready to go further than they have gone? You must gear up to precede them in succession. Like the story of Queen Vashti and Esther. Get ready to precede the Queen and do far more and beyond than what she did. You're next in Line. It's Your Time. Get Ready to add your name to the Bloodline.

Prayer Of The Day

Lord, I praise you for today. Thank you for helping me to celebrate others while waiting on my time to come. Lord, I can't believe my time is finally here. Lord, it's now time for my name to be added to the Bloodline of Women that have gone before me. Help me daily, as I fight the good fight of faith and continue the work of the Kingdom. Thank you Lord for making me ready. In Jesus name I pray, Amen

Day 24

Dropped, But Not Broken

Romans 8:18
"I consider that our present sufferings are not worth comparing with the glory that will be revealed in us."

There's an old saying. When life knocks you down, you get back up. There are times in our lives that we experience frustrations, stress and disappointments by our families, our spouses and friends. We are often feel like we have been dropped, broken and can never be repaired. In life, we as women have always gone through it. But we always need to keep in mind that 'God is the Potter and we are the clay.' God has the power to pick us back up. Not only just repair us, but also mend us back together again. Always know that life can drop us, but in God we are not broken. For he is in control. No matter what life brings, always know that what you're going through can't compare to what God has put in you. Greater is He that is in you, than He that is in the world.

Prayer Of The Day

Heavenly Father, You are my gracious and loving God that restores and heals where brokenness and disappointment occurs. Lord, I present myself to you, standing in need of restoration. I feel let down and dropped, and I am struggling to get back up. Lord, I call upon your name, and I know that you hear me and will answer me. Thank you Lord for healing and restoring me. Thank you for hearing my prayer. In Jesus name I pray, Amen.

Day 25

Woman Of Strength

Proverbs 31:17
"She girdeth her loins with strength, and strengtheneth her arms."

Diamond of Glory, you are called a Woman of Strength today. Why? Because you come from a bloodline of Strong Women. Not women necessarily full of physical strength (muscles), but full of mental and spiritual strength (girdeth). Women have equipped and or invested strength or power into a strategic part of their body. That part of their body is regarded as the seat of physical and generative power (loins). And when we don't seem to have that physical strength to draw from, we must have a strategic place that we can draw strengthen from. Strength that is going to motivate you and empower you to keep moving. When we want to become stagnant. When we want to quit and give up. When we get physically tired, but mentally and spiritual we can still go. That's the strength that we as Women have. And we come from a bloodline of them. Their testimony also gives us the encouragement and empowerment we need to go forth. All this strength comes from our Heavenly Father, through the Holy Spirit and through reading God's Word. We are indeed not without help at any time. So Diamond of Glory, you must continue to draw that strength to shine forth even when other Diamonds lose theirs.

Erica & Lewis Rutherford Jr.

Prayer Of the Day

Heavenly Father, I am reminded of the bloodline of Women who exemplify extraordinary strength. And I know that they were who they were, because of you Lord. I am reminded this day of the Diamond that I am. Lord, I recognize my need for more of you and for your strength. Lord, help me as I depend on you for help. I receive strength today, to gird up my loins and to strengthen my arms. So that I may continue to shine forth. Thank you Lord for your help. In Jesus name I pray, Amen.

Day 26

Silence At Times Is Your Friend

Proverbs 17:28
"Even a fool, when he keeps silent, is considered wise; when he closes his lips, he is considered prudent."

How many times do you Diamond of Glory out of habit, seek and find someone to tell almost everything that you do to? Specifically sharing things that are exciting or good? I personally have a habit of wanting people to know my good news. Whether I am working on something, trying something new, going to be doing something soon or immediately, going somewhere fun or exciting or just revealing my everyday events. When you habitually do something, you a lot of times don't realize that you do it. Sometimes revealing your everyday events, future plans or even deep heart's desires or thoughts, can get you in trouble. Someone can take what you've shared for themselves, and use it to their own advantage. They can take personal private details that you have shared with them and possible share them with others. This can even cause trouble for you down the road. So, 'Silence At Times Is Your Best Friend.' There are things that will happen in your life, that you should have someone to share them with. At least, one person whom you can trust and confide in. But still, you must know when to be quiet and when you can share. Everything is not meant for everyone to know. Even at times when you want to share, you must take Silence as your friend. Proverbs 17:28 reminds us that, even when a fool keeps quiet, he is considered wise. Nothing can go in or out with closed lips. Sometimes that is best. So Diamond of Glory amongst all your other friends, remember Silence as your Friend too. Know when to pull her close, and when you keep her near but can reveal too. Sometimes being silent can make a difference.

Prayer Of The Day:

Lord, I thank you for always being concerned for me, as I journey through my everyday life. Lord, I am reminded of your words to pull Silence as my friend. Father, I realize that not being careful with what I share and with whom I share things with, can work against me. So Lord, help me to know when to be silent and when to speak. Help me not to be so trusting towards people, but only trust you completely. Thank you Lord for teaching me. In Jesus name I pray, Amen.

Day 27

Your Suffering Produces Your Crown

Romans 8:17 (KJV)
"And if children, then heirs; heirs of God, and joint-heirs with Christ; if so be that we suffer with him, that we may be also glorified together. "

Jesus is our Lord and Savior; full of all glory. First, because he was God's son. Secondly, he obtained his glory through suffering amongst us during his time here on earth. Jesus' life had purpose and meaning. He was prophesized before all men and heaven. God reveal to us that his son Jesus would be born, and become Savior of our world. After he fulfilled all prophecy and his mission on earth, he returned to heaven and took his place on the right handed side of his Father in his full glory. He was well deserving of it. Especially when you look back at his story, and all he had been through. He suffered for his Crown. Therefore Diamond of Glory, you must also suffer for your Crown. For It Is Your Suffering that Produces Your Crown. You must remember this when you are going through the roughest, toughest and most challenging times of your life. You must look back unto Jesus for encouragement through the storms. Romans 8:17 says: "And if children ..." So this should prompt you to ask yourself the question: "Am I a Child of God? Once you answer this question, then you must know and understand the family line that you are a part of. The scripture goes on to say: "..., then heirs; heirs of God, and joint-heirs with Christ;....." You are a part of a lineage. You are an heir, when you are child of God. You are heirs of God and joint-heirs with Christ. What an awesome honor to be a part of such a glorious family. But the last part of that scripture states: "……; if so be that we suffer with him, that we may be also glorified together." It indeed states that if everything before is true, then you must suffer with Christ in order to glorified together with him. So you must suffer as Christ has suffered, in order to be glorified with him. What is your end reward: "A Crown!" This is what we should all long for at the end of our days, when we are called home. So Diamond of Glory, will you share in the sufferings of Christ in order to produce your Crown as a Child of God? –Selah

Prayer Of The Day

Lord, in everything that I want to do or be, help me go through the process. Be my strength in times that I am weak and want to quit. Help me to know that you are with me. Through all of the pain and suffering that I may encounter in my life, help me to remember: 'That I must suffer as you suffered in order to receive my glory and crown.' Let everything that I bring you glory, honor and the praise. In Jesus name I pray, Amen.

Day 28

A Place Of Surrender

Proverbs 3:5-6 (KJV)
"Trust in the Lord with all thine heart; and lean not unto thine own understanding. In all thy ways acknowledge him and he shall direct thy path."

The word 'Trust' is a huge word in dealing with people within the world we live in. We as people tend to put our trust in a lot of things and people. And in whom we put our trust in, tells a lot about us as a person and or whom we are allowing to step into our world. But at the end of the day, there is only one individual that we should be putting our full trust and hope. That person is Jesus Christ. We as women tend to be a little more trusting than men. We as women also tend to be more receptive to surrendering ourselves unto God. We tend to trust Him more with the various details of our lives, and the lives of our loved ones. With trust comes the surrendering of your own thoughts, ways and plans to accepting and receiving the thoughts, ways and plans of person in whom they are placing their trust in. Who is that person? Is that person truly trustworthy? Can you truly and fully submit yourself to that person? The place of Surrender requires complete trust. Can you trust Christ with your life? Or do you trust your loved one or other individual in your life more? This is a question that you Diamond of Glory must answer. To continue to shine as the Diamond you are, you must trust in the Lord with all thine heart. You must not depend or lean on your own understand. You must acknowledge Christ, which will exemplify your position of surrenderance. Then He will direct your path. Will you surrender your heart and life to Christ today?

Prayer Of The Day

Heavenly Father, I come before you right now asking that you would forgive me for trusting others more than trusting you. Please forgive me for all those I put before you. And also please forgive my lack of submission unto you. Lord, I am asking now that you would help me to remain in a place of surrenderance in my relationship with you. I am also asking that you would help me to trust you more, and to come unto you first for all my needs. I love you Lord, and I surrender my heart and life to you today. Thank you Lord for receiving me. In Jesus name I pray, Amen.

Day 29

Resting and Being Renewed

Matthew 11:28
"Come to me, all you who are weary and burdened, and I will give you rest."

Rest, is one of the elements that our bodies need as we proceed through our daily lives and activities. It's crucial to our daily health, if we are to continue functioning daily. If not, our bodies will eventually shut down, and we will be no good to ourselves nor anyone. Along with that, our bodies will not be able to heal themselves properly nor move properly through the stages of life. We all have been given destinies and purposes to fulfill. So, it is crucial that we take time away from the busyness of life to regroup, to heal, to process and to allow our bodies to refresh. This also includes our mind. Many of your journey's burdens and life's pressures consume your body. Various conditions appear in our bodies. It is either because we are either not taking the appropriate time to take care of our bodies or because of genetics that have passed down through the bloodline. But as life hits us in the various ways that it does, we have someone that we can run to get the rest that we need; both physically and spiritually. And his name is Jesus Christ. He tells us in his word: "Come to me,.." which means that you are already invited to come unto the Ultimate Healer. And His invitation is to: "all you who are weary and burdened,.." Christ already knows of your need for rest, Diamond of Glory. And he is standing waiting on you to come unto him. And His promise to you Diamond of Glory is: "and I will give you rest." Christ promises to give you rest. Rest after your daily journey. Rest so that you can be renewed, rejuvenated, revived and refreshed. God wants you to find rest in him. He wants to relieve you from that which makes you weak and weary. So Diamond of Glory, will you come find your rest in him today?

Prayer Of The Day

Lord Heavenly Father, I come before you today in order that I may find rest today. Lord, you said that I could come unto you weak and burdened and that you would supply me with rest. So Lord here I am. I receive your rest and restoration today. I also receive refreshment today that I know is only found in you. Father, thank you for the invitation to come. Thank you for receiving and restoring me. In Jesus name I pray, Amen.

Day 30

Your Work Matters to God

Colossians 3:23
"And whatsoever ye do, do *it* heartily, as to the Lord, and not unto men;"

Our Heavenly Father is the creator of the entire Universe. Everything in the World, he has created. Therefore, everything in the World belongs to him. Our houses, cars, jobs, money and etc., it all belongs to God. As a Child of God, everything about you matters to God. For he created you. He birthed you out of your Mother's womb. He created you with purpose. And he has called you to fulfill Destiny. So all you do Diamond of Glory, matters to God. As a part of living amongst this world, God understands that you must work in order to survive. He created work in the beginning of the time. He created someone that could create jobs in order that you may make the money necessary in order to survive. So, He already had you in mind. Isn't that such an awesome thing? As we work to do what is necessary in order to survive, we must also keep in mind the fact of us being Kingdom Kids. As Kingdom Kids, we must conduct ourselves as such even in our work places. We must do all we do as unto God. In everything we do, we must represent Christ. Your work, Diamond of Glory truly does matter to God. So take seriously your natural job, because all your work both naturally and spiritually.

Prayer Of The Day

Heavenly Father, I come before you in order that you may examine me. Lord, I want to repent and ask forgiveness of my attitude toward the work that I do that has not been right. Lord, I know I may not always appreciate the opportunities that have been given unto me. But now, I understand that my work does indeed matter to you. I now understand the attitude I must have in all that I do. I must do it as unto you. So Lord, help me daily to see your prospective in all I do. Thank you for reminding me of your word today. I give you thanks and praise. In Jesus name I pray, Amen.

About the Authors

Erica Rutherford is an author, minister, musician, songwriter, praise dancer, praise and worship leader, speaker, teacher residing in Central Indiana with her husband, Lewis C Rutherford Jr. Erica is a motivated driven leader that has been called to encourage and empower the people of God in this hour through her music, teachings, dance and writings. Erica and her husband are currently working on their 1st CD, 2 song collaborations and their next book 'No More Egypt.'

Erica has traveled some of the world as a classical violinist. Erica now does freelance music in the genres of gospel, inspirational and jazz. In her free time, Erica enjoys crafting, knitting, video and board games, hanging with friends, learning new things and traveling.

Erica can be reached her Facebook account name: EricaGodschildRutherford, website: www.kingdomwritersbooks.wordpress.com and email: kingdomwriters2017@gmail.com . You can visit Amazon.com, Barnes&Noble.com or contact her personally to purchase her books.

Lewis C Rutherford Jr. is an minister, singer, songwriter, musician and author residing in central Indiana with his wife Erica A Rutherford. Lewis is a high energy passionate leader that is called to encourage and empower the people of God in this hour through his music, teachings and his writings. Lewis and his wife are currently working on their 1st CD, 2 song collaborations and their next book 'No More Egypt.'

Lewis has traveled the world participating in various music conferences and events. Lewis does freelance music mainly in the genres of inspirational, gospel and jazz. In his free time, Lewis enjoys video and board games, learning and trying new things, hanging with friends, and traveling.

Lewis can be reach at his Gmail account name: Gospodj@gmail.com or kingdomwriters2017@gmail.com , and website: www.kingdomwritersbooks.wordpress.com , you can visit Amazon.com, Barnes&Noble.com or contact him personally to purchase his books.

www.ingramcontent.com/pod-product-compliance
Lightning Source LLC
Chambersburg PA
CBHW060425050426
42449CB00009B/2144